ÉVANGÉLINE

Written by
Henry Wadsworth Longfellow
in 1847

Edited by
René Babineau
in 1992

Cover : René Babineau

Cover photo   : Vermillonville
Photographer : Deal Bowie & Assoc.

Edited and illustrated by René Babineau

ISBN : 2-920726-17-X

TABLE OF CONTENTS

ILLUSTRATIONNS

I N T R O D U C T I O N

While preparing his poem Longfellow did not meet with Évangéline and Gabriel. " H.L.C.--- heard from a French Canadian a story of a young couple in Acadie. On their marriage day, all the men of the province were summoned to assemble in the churoclamation. When assembled, they were all seized and shipped off to be distributed through New England, among them the new bridegroom. His bride set off in search of him, wandered about New England all her life-time, and at last when she was old, she found her bridegroom on his death-bed. The shock was so great that it killed her likewise." (In Hawthorne's American Note-Book, under date of October 24, 1838)

Longfellow's daughter Alice wrote in 1896 : "It may have been the same H.L.C. who dined with Hawthorne and Mr. Longfellow one day and told the poet that he had been trying to persuade Hawthorne to write a story on this theme. Hawthorne said he could not see in it the material for a tale, but Longfellow at once caught at it as the suggestion for a poem." "Give it to me," he said, "and promise that you will not write about it until I have written the poem."

The poet had never been in Acadie. He wrote to a friend : " I have never been in Nova Scotia. As far as I remember, the authorities I mostly relied on in writing Évangéline were the Abbé Raynal and Mr. Haliburton ; the first for the pastoral, simple life of the Acadians ; the second for the history of their banishment. "

In 1847 when the poem was released the Acadians had never been heard of. Longfellow told the whole world of our existence, and he is still read today. Thank you Longfellow !

We find Évangéline and Gabriel in Louisiana. My first visit to St. Martinville when I saw Éméline Labiche on the tomb of Évangéline I said to myself, "It cannot be." There were no Labiche in Acadie in 1755. And while researching, I found the name in the years 1604-05. In Louisiana, I also found a plaque stating that Louis Arceneaux was the prototype of Gabriel being born in Beauséjour. On his testament, Louis says he was born in St. James Parish in Louisiana but his fathe, Pierre, was born in Beauséjour. Therefore, he can be the Gabriel. If he is the Gabriel, he must have courted girls in Beauséjour, and checking the records there I found 97 girls that he could have courted between the ages of 15 to 25. I brought those records to Louisiana and checked them against Father Hébert's genealogy books and found about a dozen that married in Louisiana but only one, Marie Cormier, that died a single girl. She was buried in Opelousas cemetery November 2nd 1800.

Pierre Arsenault, son of Jean and Anne Hébert, was born in Beauséjour in 1731, and Marie Cormier, daughter of Joseph and Marie Arsenault was born, February 18 , 1740. Pierre was 24 and Marie 15 in 1755, they could have been courting and ready to get married as this was often done those days. But as far as betrothal, this was invented by Longfellow and taken up by many Historians as fact, although it only started recently in Acadie. This has been checked by Father Anselme Chiasson and Father D'entremont. In **Religion in Life at Louisbourg, 1713-1758** by A.J.B. Johnston p. 127 : "At Louisbourg, only a single betrothal was recorded in 30 years" and they were of Noble ancestry from France.

Pierre arrived in 1765, in Cabanocée near Vacherie in Louisiana and established his family and became a farmer who raised cattle. He was then married to Anne Bergeron and in 1769 they had three daughters, Rosalie, 5 years, Marie-Jeanne, 3, and Françoise, 10 months. Their first son, Louis, was born in St. James Parish and married Anne Breau on May 9,1788. The second son, Pierre, was born January 2 nd, 1773 in the diocese of Baton Rouge. They also had Cyprien born in 1787. as well as Alexandre, and François.

Since he named his first two sons Louis and Pierre he could have been bearing the two names, but there are no documents to prove it, only that it was customary to name the first son exactly as his father was.

In 1887, we find Pierre making a notarized act before coming to Carencro with his family to establish his herd. The house on the cover of this book was taken from the site where Pierre originally built his house. This House in Vermillionville, near Lafayette, has had a face lift and is now opened to the public. It was built circa 1840 by Louis and his children and Cidalise, his daughter, and her husband lived in it for a certain time. Louis Joseph Mouton son of Cidalise bought it from his father in 1856 and sold it in 1875 to François Abadie. Seventy five years later, Thomas Arcenaux, descendant of Pierre, son of Gabriel got it back in the family and gave it to Vermillionville to be opened to the public April 1990.

Longfellow was the first one to write about the Acadians in 1847 before **Rameau de Saint Père**, a Frenchmen, who wrote their History in 1859 . In 1866, **Napoléon Bourassa**, a Quebecer, wrote in prose what Longfellow had written in poetry. In 1895, **Edouard Richard** was the first Acadian to write an Acadian History, and Pascal Poirier in 1898 added his share.

Had he been an Acadien, Longfellow, would have written a totally different poem, with more pertinent facts. However we may be thankful that he told the whole world about us and, thanks to him, **the spirits of Évangéline and Gabriel travels the Universe today.**

René Babineau B.A.; C.S.W.; B.Ed.

```
                                                                16 CORMIER, Robert____

                                          8 CORMIER, Thomas_____

                                          |B: -- -- 1636        17|PÉRAUDE, Marie
                                          |W: Port-Royal, Acadie

                      4 CORMIER, Alexis_____
                      |Marr:
                      |B: -- -- 1676        |D: -- -- 1690        18 GIROUARD, François____
                      |W: Beaubassin, Acadie |W: Beaubassin, Acadie |
                      |Marr:                9|GIROUARD, Marie-Madeleine
                      |D: -                 |B:                   19|AUCOIN, Jeanne_____
                      |W: -, Acadie         |W:
                                            D:                                    20

          2 CORMIER, Joseph_____
          |B: -- -- 1718                    10 LEBLANC, Jacques_____
          |W: Beaubassin, Acadie            |B:                                   21
          |Marr:                            |W: -,
          |D:                               |
          |W:                   5|LEBLANC, Marie_____
                                 |D:                                              22
                                 |W: Grand-Pré (B.A 910, Acadie
                                 |B: -- -- 1680        11|HÉBERT, Catherine_____
                                 |D:                   |B: -                      23|
                                 |W:                   |W: -,
                                                        D:
                                                        W:

1
CORMIER, Marie-J. Evangéline
B 18 fév 1740
W Beaubassin, Acadie
D 02 nov 1800
W Opelousas, Louisiane|
```

```
                                                                16 ARSENEAUX, Cyprien jr._
                                              8 ARSENEAUX, Hippolyte_
                                              |B: bt avr 1835        17|BREAU, Marie (La Bonne)
                                              |W: age 4 mois,
                        4 ARSENEAUX, Joseph_
                        |Marr:  01 mai 1854
                        |B:                   18 BENOIT, Augustin
                        |W:
                        |D:    01
                        9|BENOIT, Azélima_
                        |B:                   19|BABINEAU, Anastasie
                        |W: Lafayette, Louisiane
                        |D:
      2 ARSENEAUX, Elton_
      |B: 19 déc 1890
      |W:  , Louisiane
      |Marr:   10 nov 1910
      |D: 07 avr 1962
      |W:                      20 PRÉJEAN, Symphorien
                        10 PRÉJEAN, Emile_
                        |B:                   21|BREAU, Eugénie_
                        |W:
                        |D:
                        5|PRÉJEAN, Célina_
                        |Marr:                22 HÉBERT, Servin
                        |B:
                        |W:
                        |D:                   11|HÉBERT, Céleste_
                                              23|BABINEAU, Marcélite_
1
ARSENEAUX, Joseph_
B 23 fév 1912
W , Louisiane
```

16 ARSENAULT, Pierre

8 ARSENAULT, Pierre
|B: -- ---- 1676
|W: Beaubassin, Acadie
17|DUGAS, Marguerite

4 ARSENAULT, Jean
|B: -- ---- 1708
|W: Beaubassin, Acadie
|Marr: -- ---- 1730
|D:
|W:

|Marr: -- ----1697

18 BOUDROT, Charles
9|BOUDROT, Anne
|B:
|W:
19|BOURG, Renée

2 ARSENAULT, Pierre (Louis)
|B: -- ---- 1731
|W: Beaubassin, Acadie
|Marr:
|D:
|W:

10 HÉBERT, Jacques
|B: -- ---- 1710
|W: Beaubassin, Acadie

20 HÉBERT, Jean
21|DOUCET, Anne

5|HÉBERT, Anne-Marie
|B:
|W:
|D:
|W:

|Marr:
|D:
|W:
11|GAUTROT, Jeanne
|B:

22 GAUTROT, Claude

1
ARSENEAUX, Cyprien Sr.
B — --- 1787
W St James, (H.v.1 p.11)
Marr: ed: 13 mai 1805
D 20 mai 1832
W Lafayette, Louisiane
MOUTON, Marguerite Adélaide

12 BERGERON, Barthélemy
6 BERGERON, Barthélemy
|B: -- ----1698
|W: , France
|Marr:
|D:
|W:

|B: -- ---- 1664
|W: , France

23|THÉRIAULT, Marie
13|SERREAU, Geneviève
|B:
|W: St. Aubain, France

3|BERGERON, Anne
|B: -- --- 1741

7|DUGAS, Marguerite

26 ,
25

27

WILL OF PIERRE ARSENNAUX 1793

In the name of all powerful God, may those who shall see this writing know that I, Pierre Arsenaux, native of La Pointe de Beauséjour, Province of Acadie, legetimate son of Jean Arsenaux and Anne Hébert, my deceased parents, being of sound mind and possessed of a good memoroy which it has pleased God to grant me and believing fervently in the mysteries of the Holy Trinity, Father, son and Holy Spirit, and in all the truths taught by our Holy Mother, the Catholic, Apostolic, and Roman Church, guided by the Holy Spirit, in which belief I confess I have believed and wish to believe until my death, being certain that death is inevitable for all creatures and thus my incentive for the execution of this my last will and testament, which I desire shall be as follows

First, I recommend my soul to God my Soverign Lord to Him Who has given, created and redeemed same same to me at the cost of His precious blood - I beg Him to grant me pardon and life everlasting, being the reason for its creation, and when I die, it is my wish that I be buried in the parochial cemetery in a manner deemed suitable by my children. It is also my wish that my wife be so buried.

I declare that I was married, according to
the rites of Holy Church, to Anne Bergeron,
with whom I have had eight children as
follows : Louis, Pierre, Alexandre, Cyprien,
François, Rosalie, Marie, and Françoise.

I acknowledge giving to each one of my
children six arpents of land - such is my
wish.

I declare that the remaining land owned by
me, in addition to the above divided among my
children, should belong to my widow such
land to be later divided among my children,
being persuaded of their just and intelligent
accord - such is my wish.

I want it understood that, after my death,
none of my possessions shall be disposed of
except for the sole benefit of my children
and in order to insure an equal partition of
my possessions, I appoint as Trustix for my
children, Dame Anne Bergeron, my wife, and as
"Curateur", Louis Arsenaux my eldest son -
all in accordance with the law - such is my
wish.

Concerning Dame Anne Bergeron, my wife, I
request that she lives all of her life with
our children and I declare that she is
entitled to half of all the comunity property
to be found after my death - such is my wish.

I declare that I have no debts.

I declare that Sir Pre. Decuir owes me the sum recorded in the archives of this jurisdiction.

I request that the parish priest be authorized to say thirty low masses for the repose of my soul and also an anniversary requiem service. I exhort all my children and also my friends to attend the above mentioned services- such is my wish.

I constitute and name as my heirs, all of my children above named. I charge them, with all the force of my paternal love, to live all their lives in peace, in union, in accord and in the fear of God - such is my wish.

As executor of this, my last will and testament, I name Sieur Jean Bérard, inhabitant of this district, charging him to fulfill or to have fulfilled all of my wishes....

Franco Caso Y Vriengo (?)

> Sieur Pre. Arsenaux
> Jean Batiste Meloncon
> Louis Dratilly Cestia f.
> Dominique Babineau
> Cadet St. Julien

EXTRACTS FROM THE WILL

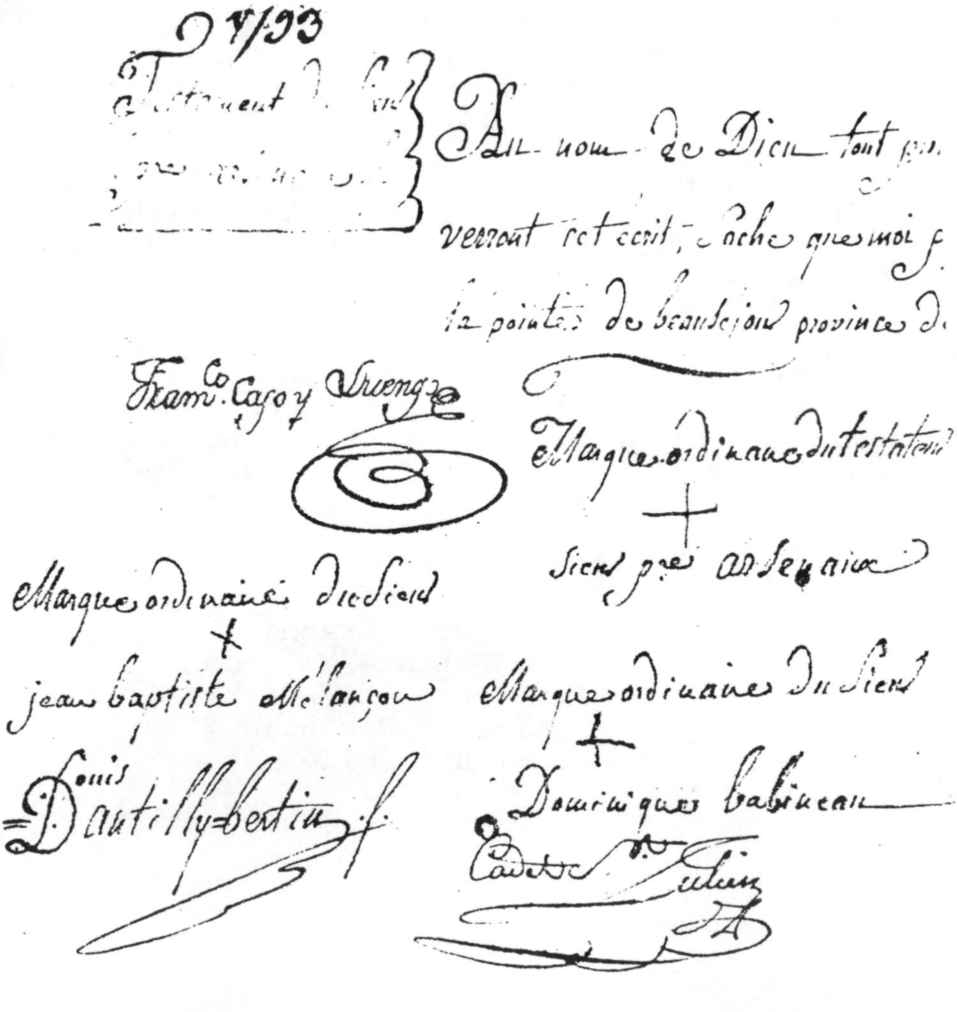

P R E L U D E

This is the forest primeval. The murmuring
     pines and the hemlocks,
Bearded with moss, and in garments green,
     indistinct in the twilight,
Stand like Druids of eld, with voices sad and
     profetic,
Stand like harpers hoar, with beards that
     rest on their bosoms.
Loud from its rocky caverns, the deep-voiced
     neighboring ocean
Speaks, and in accents disconsolate answers
     the wail of the forest.

This is the forest primeval ; but where   are
     the hearts that beneath it
Leaped   like the   roe, when   he heats   in the
     voodland the voice of the huntsman ?
Where is the thatch-roofed village,   the home
     of Acadian farmers, -
Men whose   lives glided on   like rivers   that
     water the woodlands,
Darkened by shadows of earth, but reflecting
     an image of heaven ?
Waste are those pleasant farms, and the
     farmers for ever departed !
Scattered like dust and leaves, when the
     mighty blast of October
Seize them, and   whirl them aloft,   and
     sprinkle them far o'er the ocean.
Naught but tradition remains of the
     beautiful village of Grand-Pré.

Ye who believe in affection that hopes, and
     endures, and is patient,
Ye who believe in the beauty and strength of
     woman's devotion,
List to the mournful tradition still sung by
     the pines of the forest ;
List to a Tale of Love in Acadie, home of
     of the happy.

1.

In the Acadian land, on the shores of the
    Basin of Minas,
Distant, secluded, still, the village of
    Grand-Pré
Lay in the fruitful valley. Vast meadows
    stretched to the eastward
Giving the village its name, and pasture to
    flocks without number.
Dikes, that the hands of the farmers had
    raised with labor incessant,
Shut out the turbulent tides ; but at stated
    seasons the flood-gates
Opened, and welcomed the sea to wander at
    will o'er the meadows.
West and south there were fields of flax, and
    orchards and cornfields
Spreading afar and unfenced o'er the plain ;
    and away to the northward
Blomidon rose, and the forests old, and aloft
    on the mountains
Sea-fogs pitched their tents, and mists from
    the mighty Atlantic
Looked on the happy valley, but ne'er from
    their station descended.
There, in the midst of its farms, reposed the
    Acadian village.
Strongly built were the houses, with frames
    of oak and of hemlock,
Such as the peasants of Normandy built in the

reign of the Henries.
Thatched were the roofs, with dormer-windows;
   and gables projecting
Over the basement below protected and shaded
   the doorway.
There in the tanquil evenings of summer, when
   brightly the sunset
Lighted the village street, and glided the
   vanes on the chimneys,
Matrons and maidens sat in snow-white caps
   and in kirtles
Scarlet and blue and green, with distaffs
   spinning the golden
Flax for the gossiping looms, whose noisy
   shuttles within doors
Mingled their sound with the whir of the
   wheels and the songs of the maidens.
Solemnly down the street came the parish
   priest, and the children
Paused in their play to kiss the hand he
   extended to bless them.
Reverend walked he among them ; and up rose
   matrons and maidens,
Hailing his slow approach with words of
   affectionate welcome.
Then came the laborers home from the
fields, and sereneley the sun sank
Down to his rest, and twilight prevailed.
   Anon from the belfry
Softly the Angelus sounded, and over the
   roofs of the village
Columns of pale blue smoke, like clouds of
   incense ascending,
Rose from a hundred hearths, the· homes of
   peace and contentment.
Thus dwelt together in love these simple
   Acadian farmers, -
Dewelt in the love of God and of man. Alike
   were they free from

the vice of republics.
Neither locks had they to their doors, nor
     bars to their windows ;
But their dwellings were open as day and the
     hearts of the owners ;
There the richest was poor, and the poorest
     lived in abundance.

Somewhat apart from the village, and nearer
     the Basin of Minas,
Bénédict Bellefontaine, the wealthiest farmer
     of Grand-Pré,
Dwelt on his goodly acres ; and with him,
     directing his household,
Gentle Évangéline lived, his child, and the
     pride of the village.
Stalworth and stately in form was the man of
     seventy winters ;
Hearty and hale was he, an oak that is
     covered with snow flakes ;
White as the snow were his locks, and his
     cheeks as brown as the oak-leaves.
Fair was she to behold, that maiden of
     seventeen summers ;
Black were her eyes as the berry that grows
     on the thorn by the wayside,
Black, yet how softly they gleamed beneath
     the brown shade of her tresses !
Sweet was her breath as the breath of kine
     that feed in the meadows.
When in the harvest heat she bore to the
     reapers at noontide
Flagons of home-brewed ale, ah ! fair in
     sooth was the maiden.
Fairer was she when, on Sunday morn, while
     the bell from its turret
Sprinkled with holy sounds the air, as the

priest with his hussop
Sprinkles the congregation, and scatters
blessings upon them,
Down the long street she passed, with her
chaplet of beads and her missal,
Wearing her Norman cap, and her kirtle of
blue, and the ear-rings
Brought in the olden time from France, and
since, as an heirloom,
Handed down from mother to child, through
long generations.
But a celestial brightness - a more ethereal
beauty -
Shone on her face and encircled her form,
when, after confession,
Homeward serenely she walked with God's
benediction upon her.
When she had passed, it seemed like the
ceasing of exquisite music.

Firmly builded with rafters of oak, the house
of the farmer
Stood on the side of a hill commanding the
sea ; and a shady
Sycamore grew by the door, with a woodbine
wreathing around it.
Rudely carved was the porch, with seats
beneath ; and a footpath
Led throngh an orchard wide, and disappeared
in the meadow.
Under the sycamore-tree were hives overhung
by a penthouse,
Such as the traveller sees in regions remote
by the roadside,
Built o'er a box for the poor, or the blessed
image of Mary.
Farther down, on the slope of the hill, was
the well with its moss-grown

Bucket, fastened with iron, and near it a
    trough for the horses.
Shielding the house from storms, on the
    north, were the barns and the farmyard ;
There stood the broad-wheeled wains and the
    antique ploughs and the harrows ;
There were the folds for the sheep ; and
    there, in his feathered seraglio,
Strutted the lordly turkey, and crowed the
    cock, with the selfsame
Voice that in ages of old had startled the
    penitent Peter.
Bursting with hay were the barns, themselves
    a village. In each one
Far o'er the gable projected a roof of thatch
    and a staircase,
Under the sheltering eaves, led up to the
    odorous corn-loft.
There too the dove-cot stood, with its meek
    and innocent inmates
Murmuring ever of love ; while above in the
    variant breezes
Numberless noisy weathercocks rattled and
    sang of mutation.

Thus, at peace with God and the world, the
    farmer of Grand-Pré
Lived on his sunny farm, and Évangéline
    governed his household.
Many a youth, as he knelt in the church and
    opened his missal,
Fixed his eyes upon her as the saint of his
    deepest devotion ;
Happy was he who might touch her hand or the
    hem of her garment !
Many a suitor came to her door, by the

darkness befriended,
And, as he knocked and waited to hear the
    sound of her footsteps,
Knew not which beat the louder, his heart or
    the knocker of iron ;
Or, at the joyous feast of the Patron Saint
    of the village,
Bolder grew, and pressed her hand in the
    dance as he whispered
Hurried words of love, that seemed a part of
    the music.
But, among all who came, young Gabriel only
    was welcome ;
Gabriel Lajeunesse, the son of Basil the
    blacksmith,
Who was a mighty man in the village, and
    honored of all men ;
For since the birth of time, throughout all
    ags and nations,
Has the craft of the smith been held in
    repute by the people.
Basil was Bénédict's friend. Their children
    from earliest childhood
Grew up together as brother and sister ; and
    Father Félicien,
Priest and pedagogue both in the village, had
    taught them their letters
Out of the selfsame book, with the hymns of
    the church and the plain-song.
But when the hymn was sung, and the daily
    lesson completed,
Swiftly they hurried away to the forge of
    Basil the blacksmith.
There at the door they stood, with· wondering
    eyes to behold him
Take in his leathern lap the hoof of the
    horse as a plaything,
Nailing the shoe in its place ; while near
    him the tire of the cart-wheel

Lay   like a   fiery snake,   coiled round   in a
     circle of cinders.
Oft   on   autumnal eves,   when without   in the
     gathering darkness
Bursting with   light   seemed   the   smithy,
     through every cranny and crevice,
Warm by the   forge within they watched the
     laboring bellows,
And as   its panting ceased, and the sparks
     expired in the ashes,
Merrily laughed,   and said they were nuns
     going into the chapel.
Oft on sledges in winter, as swift as the
     swoop of the eagle,
Down the hillside bounding, they glided away
     o'er the meadow.
Oft in the barns they climbed to the populous
     nests on the rafters,
Seeking with eager eyes that wondrous stone,
     which the swallow
Brings from the shore of the sea to restore
     the sight of its fledglings ;
Lucky was he who found that stone in the nest
     of the swallow !
Thus   passed a few   swift years,   and they no
     longer were children.
He was a valiant youth, an his face, like
     the face of the morning,
Gladdened the earth with its light, and
     ripened thought into action.
She was a woman now, with the heart and hopes
     of a woman.
"Sunshine of Saint Eulalie" was she called ;
     for that was the sunshine
Which, as the farmers believed, would load
     their orchards with apples ;
She, too, would bring to her husband's house

delight and abundance,
Filling it full of love and the ruddy faces
of children.

11.

Now had the season returned, when the nights
      grow colder and longer,
And the retreating sun the sign of the
      Scorpion enters.
Birds of passage sailed through the leaden
      air from the ice-bound,
Desolate northern bays to the shores of
      tropical islands.
Harvests were gathered in ; and wild with
      the winds of September
Wrestled the trees of the forest, as Jacob of
      old with the angel.
All the signs foretold a winter long and
      inclement.
Bees, with prophetic instinct of want, had
      hoarded their honey
Till the hive overflowed ; and the Indian
      hunters asserted
Cold would the winter be, for thick was the
      fur of the foxes.
Such was the advent of autunm. Then followed
      that beautiful season,
Called by the pious Acadian peasants the
      Summer of All-Saints !
Filled was the air with a dreamy and magical
      light ; and the landscape

Lay as if new-created in all the freshness of
    childhood.
Peace seemed to reign upon earth, and the
    restless heart of the ocean
Was for a moment consoled. All sounds were in
    harmony blended.
Voices of children at play, the crowing of
    cocks in the farm-yards,
Whir of wings in the drowsy air, and the
    cooing of pigeons,
All were subdued and low as the murmurs of
    love and the great sun
Looked with the eye of love through the
    golden vapors around him ;
While arrayed in its robes of russet and
    scarlet and yellow,
Bright with the sheen of the dew, each
    glittering tree of the forest
Flashed like the plane-tree the Persian
    adorned with mantles and jewels.

Now recommenced the reign of rest and
    affection and stillness.
Day with its burden and heat had departed,
    and twilight descending
Brought back the evening star to the sky, and
    the herds to the homestead,
Pawing the ground they came, and resting
    their necks on each other,
And with their nostrils distended inhaling
    the freshness of evening.
Foremost, bearing the bell, Évangéline's
    beautiful heifer,
Proud of her snow-white hide, and the ribbons
    that waved from her collar,
Quietly paced and slow, as if conscious of
    human affection.
Then came the shepherd back with his bleating

flocks from the seaside,
Where was their favorite pasture. Behind them
    followed the watch-dog,
Patient, full of importance, and grand in the
    pride of his instinct,
Walking from side to side with a lordly air,
    and superbly
Waving his huysky tail, and urging forward
    the stragglers ;
Regent of flocks was he when the shepherd
    slept ; their protector,
When from the forest at night, through the
    starry silence, the wolves howled.
Late, with the rising moon, returned the
    wains from the marshes,
Laden with briny hay, that filled the air
    with its odor.
Cheerily neighed the steeds, with dew on
    their manes and their fetlocks,
While aloft on their shoulders the wooden and
    penderous saddles,
Painted with brilliant dyes, and adorned with
    tassels of crimson,
Nodded in bright array, like hollyhocks heavy
    with blossoms.
Patiently stood the cows meanwhile, and
    yielded their udders
Unto the milkmaid's hand ; whilst loud and in
    regular cadence
Into the sounding pails the foaming
    streamlets descended.
Lowing of cattle and peals of laughter were
    heard in the farm-yard,
Echoed back by the barns. Anon they sank into
    stillness ;
Heavily closed, with a jarring sound, the
    valves of the barn-doors,
Rattled the wooden bars, and all for a season

was silent.

In-doors, warm by the wide-mouthed fireplace,
    idly the farmer
Sat in his elbow-chair, and watched how the
    flames and the smoke-wreaths
Struggled together like foes in a burning
    city. Behind him,
Nodding and mocking along the wall with
    gestures fantastic,
Darted his own huge shadow, and vanished
    away into darkness.
Faces, clumsily carved in oak, on the back of
    his arm-chair
Laughed in the flickering light, and the
    pewter plates on the dresser
Caught and reflected the flame, as shields of
    armies the sunshine.
Fragments of songs the old man sang, and
    carols of Christmas,
Such as at home, in the olden time, his
    fathers before him
Sang in their Norman orchards and bright
    Burgundian vineyards.
Close at her father's side was the gentle
    Évangéline seated,
Spinning flax for the loom, that stood in the
    corner behind her.
Silent awhile were its treadles, at rest was
    its diligent shuttle,
While the monotonous drone of the wheel, like
    the drone of a bagpipe,
Followed the old man's song, and united the
    fragments together.
As in a church, when the chant of the choir
    at intervals ceases,
Footfalls are heard in the aisles, or words
    of the priest at the altar,
So, in each pause of the song, with measured

motion the clock clicked.

Thus as they sat, there were footsteps heard,
     and, suddenly lifted,
Sounded the wooden latch, and the door swung
     back on its hinges.
Bénédict knew by the hob-nailed shoes it was
     Basil the blacksmith,
And by her beating heart Évangéline knew who
     was with him.
"Welcome !" the   farmer exclaimed, as their
     footsteps paused on the threshold,
"Welcome, Basil, my friend ! Come, take thy
     place on the settle
Close by the chimney-side, which is always
     empty without thee ;
Take from the shelf overhead thy pipe and the
     box of tobacco ;
Never so much thyself art thou as when,
     through the curling
Smoke of the pipe or the forge, thy friendly
     and jovial face gleams
Round and red as the harvest moon through the
     mist of the marshes."
Then, with a smile of content, thus answered
     Basil the blacksmith,
Taking with easy air thy accustomed seat by
     the fireside : -
"Bénédict Bellefontaine, thou hast ever thy
     jest and thy ballad !
Ever in cheerfullest mood art thou, when
     others are filled with
Gloomy forebodings of ill, and see only ruin
     before them.
Happy art thou, as if every day thou hadst
     picked up a horseshoe."
Pausing a moment, to take the pipe that

Évangéline brought him,
And with a coal from the embers had lighted,
   he slowly continued : -
"Four days now are passed since the English
   ships at their anchors
Ride in the Gaspereau's mouth, with their
   cannon pointed against us.
What their design may be is unknown ; but all
   are commanded
On the morrow to meet in the church, where
   his Majesty's mandate
Will be proclaimed as law in the land. Alas !
   in the mean time
Many surmises of evil alarm the hearts of the
   people."
Then made answer the farmer : -   "Perhaps
   some friendlier purpose
Brings these ships to our shores. Perhaps the
   harvests in England
By   untimely rains or untimelier heat have
   been blighted,
And from our bursting barns they would feed
   their cattle and children."
"Not so thinketh the folk in the village,"
   said warmly, the blacksmith,
Shaking his head, as in doubt ; then, heaving
   a sigh, he continued : -
"Louisbourg is not forgotten, nor Beauséjour,
   nor Port-Royal.
Many already have fled to the forest, and
   lurk on its outskirts,
Waiting with anxious hearts the dubious fate
   of tomorrow.
Arms have been taken from us, and warlike
   weapons of all kinds ;
Nothing is left but the blacksmith's sledge
   and the scythe of the mower."
Then with a pleasant smile made answer the
   jovial farmer : -

"Safer are we unarmed, in the midst of our
   flocks and our cornfields,
Safer within these peaceful dikes, besieged
   by the enemy's cannon.
Fear no evil, my friend, and to-night may no
   shadow of sorrow
Fall on this house and hearth ; for this is
   the night of the contract.
Built are the house and the barn. The merry
   lads of the village
Strongly have built them and well ; and,
   breaking the glebe roud about them,
Filled the barn with hay, and the house with
   food for a twelvemonth.
René LeBlanc will be here anon, with his
   papers and inkhorn.
Shall we not then be glad, and rejoice in the
   joy of our children ?"
As apart by the window she stood, with her
   hand in her lover's,
Blushing Évangéline heard the words that her
   father had spoken,
And, as they died on his lips the worthy
   notary entered.

111.

Bent like a laboring oar, that toils in the
    surf of the ocean,
Bent, but not broken, by age was the form of
    the notary public ;
Shocks of yellow hair, like the silken floss
    of the maize, hung
Over his shoulders ; his forehead was high ;
    and glasses with horn bows
Sat astride on his nose, with a look of
    wisdom supernal.
Father of twenty children was he, and more
    than a hundred
Children's children rode on his knee, and
    heard his great watch tick.
Four long years in the times of the war had
    he languished a captive,
Suffering much in an old French fort as the
    friend of the English.
Now, though warier grown, without all guile
    or suspicion,
Ripe in wisdom was he, but patient, and
    simple, and childlike.
He was beloved by all, and most of all by the
    children ;
For he told them   tales of the Loup-garou in
    the forest,
And the goblin that came in the night to

water the horses,
And of the white Létiche, the ghost of a
    child who unchristened
Died, and was doomed to haunt unseen the
    chambers of children ;
And how on Christmas eve the oxen talked in
    the stable,
And how the fever was cured by a spider shut
    up in a nutshell,
And of the marvellous powers of four-leaved
    clover and horseshoes,
With whatsoever else was writ in the lore of
    the village.
Then up rose from his seat by the fireside
    Basil the blacksmith,
Knocked from his pipe the ashes, and slowly
    extending his right hand,
"Father LeBlanc," he exclaimed, "thou hast
    heard the talk in the village,
And, perchance, canst tell us some news of
    these ships and their errand."
Then with modest demeanor made answer the
    notary public, -
"Gossip enough have I heard, in sooth, yet am
    never the wiser ;
And what their errand may be I know not
    better than others.
Yet am I not of those who imagine some evil
    intention
Bring them here, for we are at peace ; and
    why then molest us ?
"God's name !" shouted the hasty and somewhat
    irascible blacksmith ;
"Must we in all things look for the how, and
    the why, and the wherefore ?
Daily injustice is done, and might is the
    right of the strongest !"
But, without heeding his warmth, continued

the notary public, -
"Man is unjust, but God is just ; and finally justice
Triumphs ; and well I remember a story, that often consoled me,
When as a captive I lay in the old French fort at Port-Royal."
This was the old man's favorite tale, and he loved to repeat it
When his   neighbors complained   that any injustice was done them.
"Once in an   ancient city, whose name I no longer remember,
Raised aloft on a column, a brazen statue of Justice
Stood in the public square, upholding the scales in its left hand,
And in its right a sword, as an emblem that justice presided
Over the laws of the land, and the hearts and homes of the people.
Even the birds had built their nests in the scales of the balance,
Having no fear of the sword that flashed in the sunshine above them.
But in the course of time the laws of the land were corrupted ;
Might took the place of right, and the weak were oppressed, and the mighty
Ruled with an iron rod. Then it chanced in a noblemAn's palace
That a necklace of pearls was lost, and ere long a suspicion
Fell on an orphan girl who lived as maid in the household.
She, after form of trial condemned to die on the scaffold,
Patiently met her doom at the foot of the statue of Justice.

As to her Father in heaven her innocent
    spirit ascended,
Lo ! o'er the city a tempest rose ; and the
    bolts of the thunder
Smote the statue of bronze, and hurled in
    wrath from its left hand
Down on the pavement below the clattering
    scales of the balance,
And in the hollow thereof was found the nest
    of a magpie,
Into whose clay-built walls the necklace of
    pearls was inwoven. "
Silenced, but not convinced, when the story
    was ended, the blacksmith
Stood like a man who fain would speak but
    findeth no language ;
All his thoughts were congealed into lines on
    his face, as the vapors
Freeze in fantastic shapes on the window-
    panes in the winter.

Then Évangéline lighted the brazen lamp on
    the table,
Filled, till it overflowed, the pewter
    tankard with home-brewed
Nut-brown ale, that was famed for its stength
    in the village of Grand-Pré ;
While from his pocket the notary drew his
    papers and ink-horn,
Wrote with a steady hand the date and the age
    of the parties,
Naming the dower of the bride in flocks of
    sheep and in cattle.
Orderly all things proceeded, and duly and
    well were completed,
And the great seal of the law was set like a
    sun on the margin.

Then from his leathern pouch the farmer threw
    on the table
Three times the old man's fee in solid pieces
    of silver ;
And the notary rising, and blessing the bride
    and the bridegroom,
Lifted aloft the tankard of ale and drank to
    their welfare.
Wiping the foam from his lip, he solemnly
    bowed and departed,
While in silence the others sat and mused by
    the fireside,
Till Évangéline brought the draught-board out
    of its corner.
Soon was the game begun. In friendly
    contention the old men
Laughed at each lucky hit, or unsuccessful
    manoeuvre,
Laughed when a man was crowned, or a breach
    was made in the king-row.
Meanwhile apart, in the twilight gloom of a
    window's embrasure,
Sat the lovers, and whispered together,
    beholding the moon rise
Over the pallid sea and the silvery mist of
    the meadows.
Silently, one by one, in the infinite meadows
    of heaven,
Blossomed the lovely stars, the forget-me-
    nots of the angels.

Thus passed the evening away. Anon the bell
    from the belfry
Rang out the hour of nine, the village
    curfew, and straightway
Rose the guests and departed ; and silence
    reigned in the household.
Many a farewell word and sweet good-night on

the door-step
Lingered long in Évangéline's heart, and
    filled it with gladness.
Carefully then were covered the embers that
    glowed on the hearth-stone,
And on the oaken stairs resounded the tread
    of the farmer.
Soon with a soundless step the foot of
    Évangéline followed.
Up the staircase moved a luninous space in
    the darkness,
Lighted less by the lamp than the shining
    face of the maiden.
Silent she passed through the hall, and
    entered the door of her chamber.
Simple that chamber was, with its curtains of
    white, and its clothes-press
Ample and high, on whose spacious shelves
    were carefully folded
Linen and woollen sutffs, by the hand of
    Évangéline woven.
This was the precious dower she would bring
    to her husband in marriage,
Better than flocks and herds, being proofs of
    her skill as a housewife.
Soon she extinguished her lamp, for the
    mellow and radiant moonlight
Streamed through the windows, and lighted the
    room till the heart of the maiden
Swelled and obeyed its power, like the
    tremulous tides of the ocean.
Ah ! she was fair, exceeding fair to behold,
    as she stood with
Naked snow-white feet on the gleaming floor
    of her chamber !
Little she dreamed that below, among the
    trees of the orchard,
Waited her lover and watched for the gleam of

her lamp and her shadow.
Yet were her thoughts of him, and at times a
    feeling of sadness
Passed o'er her soul, as the sailing shade of
    clouds in the moonlight
Flitted across the foor and darkened the room
    for a moment.
And, as she gazed from the window, she saw
    serenely the moom pass
Forth from the folds of a cloud, and one star
    follow her footsteps,
As out of Abraham's tent young Ishmael
    wandered with Hagar !

IV.

Pleasantly rose next morn the sun on the
    village of Grand-Pré.
Pleasantly gleamed in the soft, sweet air the
    Basin of Minas,
Where the ships, with their wavering shadows,
    were riding at anchor.
Life had long been astir in the village, and
    clamorous labor
Knocked with its hundred hands at the golden
    gates of the morning.
Now from the country around, from the farms
    and the neighboring hamlets,
Came in their holiday dresses the blithe
    Acadian peasants.
Many a glad good-morrow and jocund laugh from
    the young folk
Made the bright air brighter, as up from the
    numerous meadows,
Where no path could be seen but the track of
    wheels in the greensward,
Group after group appeared, and joined, or
    passed on the highway.
Long ere noon, in the village all souds of
    labor were silenced.
Thronged were the streets with people ; and
    noisy groups at the house-doors
Sat in the cheerful sun, and rejoiced and
    gossiped together.
Every house was an inn, where all were
    welcomed and feasted ;
For with this simple people, who lived like

brothers together,
All things were held in common,   and what one
    had was another's.
Yet under Bénédict's   roof hospitality seemed
    more abundant :
For Évangéline   stood among the guests of her
    father ;
Bright was her face with smiles, and words of
    welcome and gladness
Fell from her beautiful lips, and blessed the
    cup as she gave it.

Under the open sky, in the odorous air of the
    orchard,
Stripped of its golden fruit, was spread   the
    feast of bethrothal.
There in   the   shade of   the   porch were   the
    priest and the notary seated ;
There good Bénédict sat, and sturdy Basil the
    blacksmith.
Not far   withdrawn from these, by   the cider-
    press and the beeehives,
Michael   the fiddler   was   placed,   with   the
    gayest of hearts and of waistcoats.
Shadow and light from the   leaves alternately
    played on his snow-white
Hair, as it waved in   the wind, and the jolly
    face of the fiddler
Glowed like a living coal when   the ashes are
    blown from the embers.
Gayly the old man   sang to the vibrant   sound
    of his fiddle,
Tous   les   Bourgeois de   Chartres,   and   **Le
    Carillon de Dunkerque,**
And anon, with his wooden shoes   beat time to
    the music.
Merrily,   merrily whirled   the wheels   of the
    dizzying dances

Under the orchard-trees and down the paths to
    the meadows ;
Old folk and young together, and children
    mingled among them.
Fairest of all the maids was Évangéline,
    Bénédict's daughter !
Noblest of all the youths was Gabriel, son of
    the blacksmith !

So passed the morning away. and lo ! with a
    summons sonorous
Sounded the bell from its tower, and over the
    meadows a drum beat.
Thronged ere long was the church with men.
    Without, in the churchyard,
Waited the women. They stood by the graves,
    and hung on the headstones
Garlands of autumn leaves and evergreens
    fresh from the forest.
Then came the guard from the ships, and
    marching proudly among them
Entered the sacred portal. With loud and
    dissonant clangor
Echoed the sound of their brazen drums from
    ceiling and casement, -
Echoed a moment only, and slowly the
    ponderous portal
Closed, and in silence the crowd awaited the
    will of the soldiers.
Then uprose their commander, and spake from
    the steps of the altar,
Holding aloft in his hands, with its seals,
    the royal commission.
"You are convened this day," he said, "by his
    Majesty's orders.
Clement and kind has he been ; but how you
    have answered his kindness,

Let you own hearts reply ! To my natural meke
    and my temper
Painful the task is I do, wich to you I know
    must be grievous.
Yet must I bow and obey, and deliver the will
    of our monarch ;
Namely, that all your lands, and dwellings,
    and cattle of all kinds
Forfeited be to the crown ; and that you
    yourselves from this province
Be transported to other lands. God grant you
    may dwell there
Ever as faithful   subjects, a happy and
    peaceable people !
Prisoners now I declare you ; for such is his
    Mahesty's pleasure !"
As, when the air is serene in the sultry
    solstice of summer,
Suddenly gathers a storm, and the deadly
    sling of the hailstones
Beats down the farmer's corn in the field and
    shatters his windows,
Hiding the sun, and strewing the ground with
    thatch from the house-roofs,
Bellowing fly the herds, and seek to break
    their enclosures ;
So on the hearts of the people descended the
    words of the speaker.
Silent a moment they stood in speechless
    wonder, and then rose
Louder and ever louder a wail of sorrows and
    anger,
And, by one impulse moved, they madly rushed
    to the door-way.
Vain was the hope of escape ; and cries and
    fierce imprecations
Rang through the house of prayer ; and high
    o'er the heads of the others
Rose, with his arms uplifted, the figure of

          Basil the blacksmith,
As, on a stormy sea, a spar is tossed by the
     billows.
Flushed was his face and distorted with
     passion ; and wildly he shouted, -
"Down with the tyrants of England ! we never
     have sworn them allegiance !
Death to these foreign soldiers, who seize on
     our homes and our harvests !"
More   he fain would have said, but the
     merciless hand of a soldier
Smote him upon the mouth, and dragged him
     down to the pavement.
In the midst of the strife and tumult of
     angry contention,
Lo ! the door of the chancel opened, and
     Father Félicien
Entered, with serious mien, and ascended the
     steps of the altar.
Raising his reverend hand, with a gesture he
     awed into silence
All that clamorous throng ; and thus he spake
     to his people ;
Deep were his tones and solemn ; in accents
     measured and mournful
Spake he, as, after the tocsin's alarum,
     distinctly the clock strikes.
"What is this that ye do, my children ? what
     madness has seized you ?
Forty years of my life have I labored among
     you, and taught you,
Not in word alone, but in deed, to love one
     another !
Is this the fruit of my toils, of my vigils
     and prayers and privations ?
Have you so soon forgotten all lessons of
     love and forgiveness ?
This is the house of the Prince of Peace, and

would you profane it
Thus with violent deeds and hearts
overflowing with hatred ?
Lo ! where the crucified Christ from his
cross is gazing upon you !
See ! in those sorrowful eyes what meekness
and holy compassion !
Hark ! how those lips still repeat the
prayer, `O Father, forgive them !'
Let us repeat that prayer in the hour when
the wicked assail us,
Let us repeat it now, and say, `O Father,
forgive them !
Few were his words of rebuke, but deep in the
hearts of his people
Sank they, and sobs of contrition succeeded
the passionate outbreak ;
While they repeated his prayer, and said, " O
Father, forgive them !"

Then came the evening service. The tapers
gleamed from the altar
Fervent and deep was the voice of the priest,
and the people responded,
Not with their lips alone, but their hearts ;
and the Ave Maria
Sang they, and fell on their knees, and their
souls, with devotion translated,
Rose on the ardor of prayer, like Elijah
ascending to heaven.

Meanwhile had spread in the village the
tidings of ill, and on all sides
Wandered, wailing, from house to house the
women and children.
Long at her father's door Évangéline stood,
with her right hand

Shielding her eyes from the level rays of the
     sun, that, descending,
Lighted the village   street with   mysterious
     splendor, and roofed each
Peasant's   cottage   with golden   thatch,   and
     emblazoned its windows.
Long within had been spread the snow-white
     cloth on the table ;
There stood the wheaten loaf, and the honey
     fragrant with wild flowers ;
There stood   the   tankard of ale,   and   the
     cheese fresh brought from the dairy,
And at the head of the board the great arm-
     chair of the farmer.
Thus did Évangéline wait at her father's
     door, as the sunset
Threw the long shadows of trees o'er the
     broad ambrosial meadows.
Ah ! on her spirit within a deeper shadow had
     fallen,
And from the fields of her soul a fragrance
     celestial ascended, -
Charity,   meekness, love   and hope,   and
     forgiveness, and patience !
Then, all-forgetful of self, she wandered
     into the village,
Cheering with looks and words the mournful
     hearts of the women,
As o'er the darkening fields with lingering
     steps they departed,
Urged by their household cares, and the weary
     feet of their children.
Down sank the great red sun, and in golden,
     glimmering vapors
Veiled the light of his face, like the
     Prophet descending from Sinai.
Sweetly over the village the bell of the
     Angelus sounded.

Meanwhile, amid the gloom, by the church
    Évangéline lingered.
All was silent within ; and in vain at the
    door and the windows
Stood she, and listened and looked, until,
    overcome by emotion,
"Gabriel !" cried she aloud with tremulous
    voice ; but no answer
Came from the graves of the dead, nor the
    gloomier grave of the living.
Slowly at length she returned to the
    tenantless house of her father.
Smouldered the fire on the hearth, on the
    board stood the supper untasted,
Empty and drear was each room, and haunted
    with phantoms of terror.
Sadly echoed her step on the stair and the
    floor of her chamber.
In the dead of the night she heard the
    disconsolate rain fall
Loud on the withered leaves of the sycamore-
    tree by the window.
Keenly the lightning flashed ; and the voice
    of the echoing thunder
Told her that God was in heaven, and governed
    the world He created !
Then she remembered the tale she had heard of
    the justice of heaven ;
Soothed was her troubled soul, and she
    peacefully slumbered till morning.

V.

Four   times the sun had risen   and set ; and
     now on the fifth day
Cheerily   called   the   cock to   the   sleeping
     maids of the farmhouse.
Soon o'er   the yellow   fields, in   silent and
     mournful procession,
Came   from the neighboring   hamlets and farms
     the Acadian women,
Driving   in ponderous   wains their   household
     goods to the sea-shore,
Pausing and looking back to gaze once more on
     their dwellings,
Ere they were shut from sight   by the winding
     road and the woodland.
Close   at their sides their children ran, and
     urged on the oxen,
While in their little hauds they clasped some
     fragments of playthings.

Thus to the Gaspereau's   mouth they hurried ;
     there on the sea-beach
Piled in confusion lay the household goods of
     the peasants.
All day long between the shore   and the ships
     did the boats ply ;
All   day long   the   wains came   laboring down
     from the village.
Late in the afternoon, when the   sun was near

to his setting,
Echoed far o'er the fields came the roll of
    drums from the churchyard.
Tither the women and children thronged. On a
    sudden the church-doors
Opened, and forth came the   guard, and
    marching in gloomy procession
Followed the long-imprisoned, but patient,
    Acadian farmers.
Even as pilgrims, who journey afar from their
    homes and their country,
Sing as they go, and in singing forget they
    are weary and wayworn,
So with songs on their lips the Acadian
    peasants descended
Down from the church to the shore, amid their
    wives and their daughters.
Foremost the young men came ; and, raising
    together their voices,
Sang with tremuilous lips a chant of the
    Catholic Missions : -
"Sacred   Heart   of   the   Saviour   ! "   O
    inexhaustible fountain !
Fill our hearts this day with strength and
    submission and patience !"
Then the old men, as they marched, and the
    women that stood by the wayside
Joined in the sacred psalm, and the birds in
    the sunshine above them
Mingled their notes therewith, like voices of
    spirits departed.

Half-way down to the shore Évangéline waited
    in silence,
Not overcome with grief, but strong in the
    hour of affliction, -
Calmly and sadly she waited, until the
    procession approached her,

And she beheld the face of Gabriel pale with
     emotion.
Tears   then   filled   her   eyes,   and   eagerly
     running to meet him,
Clasped she his hands, and laid her head on
     his shoulder, and whispered, -
"Gabriel ! be of good cheer ! for if we love
     one another,
Nothing,   in   truth,   can harm   us,   whatever
     mischances may happen !"
Smiling she spake those words ; then suddenly
     paused, for her father
Saw she slowly advancing. Alas ! how changed
     was his aspect !
Gone   was the   glow from   his cheek,   and the
     fire from his eye, and his footstep
Heavier seemed with the weight of the weary
     heart in his bosom.
But with a smile and a sigh, she clasped his
     neck and embraced him,
Speaking words of endearment where words of
     comfort availed not.
Thus to the Gaspereau's mouth moved on that
     mournful procession.

There disorder prevailed, and the tumult and
     stir of embarking.
Busily plied the freighted boats ; and in the
     confusion
Wives   were   torn   from   their   husbands, and
     mothers, too late, saw their children
Left on the land, extending their arms, with
     wildest entreaties.
So unto separate ships were Basil and Gabriel
     carried,
While   in   despair   on   the   shore Évangéline
     stood with her father.

Half the task was not done when the sun went
    down, and the twilight
Deepened and darkness around ; and in haste
    the refluent ocean
Fled away from the shore, and left the line
    of the sand-beach
Covered with waifs of the tide, with kelp and
    the slippery seaweed.
Farther back in the midst of the household
    goods and the wagons,
Like to a gypsy camp, or a leaguer after a
    battle,
All escape cut off by the sea, and the
    sentinels near them,
Lay encamped for the night the houseless
    Acadian farmers.
Back to its nethermost caves retreated the
    bellowing ocean,
Dragging adown the beach the rattling
    pebbles, and leaving
Inland and far up the shore the stranded
    boats of the sailors.
Then, as the night descended, the herds
    returned from their pastures ;
Sweet was the moist still air with the odor
    of milk from their udders ;
Lowing they waited, and long, at the well-
    known bars of the farmyard, -
Waited and looked in vain for the voice and
    the hand of the milkmaid.
Silence reigned in the streets ; from the
    church no Angelus sounded,
Rose no smoke from the roofs, and gleamed no
    lights from the windows.

But on the shore meanwhile the evening fires
    had been kindled,
Built on the drift-wood thrown on the sands

from wrecks in the tempest.
Round them shapes of gloom and sorrowful
    faces were gathered.
Voices of women were heard, and of men, and
    the crying of children.
Onward from fire to fire, as from hearth to
    hearth in his parish,
Wandered the faithful priest, consoling and
    blessing and cheering,
Like unto shipwrecked Paul on Melita's
    desolate seashore.
Thus he approached the place where Évangéline
    sat with her father,
And in the flickering light beheld the face
    of the old man,
Haggard and hollow and wan, and without
    either thought or emotion,
E'en as the face of a clock from which the
    hands have been taken.
Vainly Évangéline strove with words and
    caresses to cheer him,
Vainly offered him food ; yet he moved not,
    he looked not, he spake not,
But, with a vacant stare, ever gazed at the
    flickering fire-light.
"Benedicite !" murmured the priest, in tones
    of compassion.
More he fain would have said, but his heart
    was full, and his accents
Faltered and paused on his lips, as the feet
    of a child on a threshold,
Hushed by the scene he beholds, and the awful
    presence of sorrow.
Silently, therefore, he laid his hand on the
    head of the maiden,
Raising his eyes, full of tears, to the
    silent stars that above them
Moved on their way, unperturbed by the wrongs

and sorrows of mortal,
Then sat he down at her side, and they wept
    together in silence.

Suddenly rose from the south a light, as in
    autumn the blood-red
Moon climbs the crystal walls of heaven, and
    o'er the horizon
Titan-like stretches its hundred hands upon
    mountain and meadow,
Seizing the rocks and the rivers, and piling
    huge shadows together.
Broader and ever broader it gleamed on the
    roofs of the village,
Gleamed on the sky and the sea, and the ships
    that lay in the roadstead.
Columns of shining smoke uprose, and flashes
    of flame were
Thrust through their folds and withdrawn,
    like the quivering hands of a martyr.
Then as the wind seized the gleeds and the
    burninng thatch, and uplifting,
Whirled then aloft through the air, at once
    from a hundred house-tops
Started the sheeted smoke with flashes of
    flame intermingled.

These things behold in disimay the crowd on
    the shore and on shipboard.
Speechless at first they stood, then cried
    aloud in their anguish,
"We shall behold no more our homes in the
    village of Grand-Pré !"
Loud on a sudden the cocks began to crow in
    the farmyards,
Thinking the day had dawned ; an anon the
    lowing of cattle

Came on the evening breeze, by the barking of
    dogs interrupted.
Then rose a sound of dread, such as startles
    the sleeping incampments
Far in the western prairies or forests that
    skirt the Nebraska,
When the wild horses affrighted swept by with
    the speed of the wirlwind,
Or the loud bellowing herds of buffaloes rush
    to the river.
Such was the sound that arose on the night,
    as the herds and the horses
Broke through their folds and fences, and
    madly rushed o'er the meadows.

Overwhelmed with the sight, yet speechless,
    the priest and the maiden
Gazed on the scene of terror that reddened
    and widened before them ;
And as they turned at length to speak to
    their silent companion,
Lo ! from his seat he had fallen, and
    stretched abroad on the seashore
Motionless lay his form, from which the soul
    had departed.
Slowly the priest uplifted the lifeless
    head, and the maiden
Knelt at her father's side, and wailed aloud
    in her terror.
Then in a swoon she sank, and lay with her
    head on his bosom.
Through the long night she lay in deep,
    oblivious slumber ;
And when she woke from the trance, she beheld
    a multitude near her,
Pallid, with tearful eyes, and looks of
    saddest compassion.

Still the blaze of the burning village
    illumined the landscape,
Reddened the sky overhead, and gleamed on the
    faces around her,
And like the day of doom it seemed to her
    wavering senses.
Then a familiar voice she heard, as it said
    to the people, -
"Let us bury him here by the sea. When a
    happier season
Brings us again to our homes from the unknown
    land of our exile,
Then shall his sacred dust be piously laid in
    the churchyard."
Such were the words of the priest. And there
    in haste by the seaside,
Having the glare of the burning village for
    funeral torches,
But without bell or book, they buried the
    farmer of Grand-Pré.
And as the voice of the priest repeated the
    service of sorrow,
Lo ! with a mournful soud, like the voice of
    a vast congregation,
Solemnly answered the sea, and mingled its
    roar with the dirges.
"T'was the returning tide, that afar from the
    waste of the ocean,
With the first dawn of the day, came heaving
    and hurrying landward.
Then recommenced one more the stir and noise
    of embarking ;
And with the ebb of that tide the ships
    sailed out of the harbor,
Leaving behind them the dead on the shore,
    and the village in ruins.

PART THE SECOND

1.

Many a weary year had passed since the
     burning of Grand-Pré,
When on the falling tide the freighted
     vessels departed,
Bearing a nation, with all its household
     goods, into exile,
Exile without an end, and without an example
     in story.
Far asunder, on separate coasts, the Acadians
     landed ;
Scattered were they, like flakes of snow,
     when the wind from the north-east
Strikes aslant through the fogs that darken
     the Banks of Newfoundland.
Friendless, homeless, hopeless, they wandered
     from city to city,
From the cold lakes of the North to sultry
     southern savannas, -

From the bleak shores of the sea to the lands
       where the father of waters
Seizes the hills in his hands, and drags them
       down to the ocean,
Deep   in   their sands to bury the scattered
       bones of the mammoth.
Friends they   sought   and homes ; and many,
       despairing, heart-broken,
Asked of the earth but a grave, and no longer
       a friend nor a fireside.
Written   their history   stands on   tablets of
       stone in the churchyards.
Long among them was seen a maiden who waited
       and wandered,
Lowly and meek in spirit, and patiently
       suffering all things.
Fair was she and young : but, alas ! before
       her extended,
Dreary and vast and silent, the desert of
       life, with its pathway
Marked by the graves of those who had
       sorrowed and suffered before her,
Passions long extinguished, and hopes long
       dead and abandoned,
As the emigrant's way o'er the western desert
       is marked by
Camp-fire long consumed,   and bones that
       bleach in the sunshine.
Something there was in her life incomplete,
       imperfect, unfinished ;
As if a morning of June, with all its music
       and sunshine,
Suddenly paused in th sky, and, fading,
       slowly descended
Into the east again, from whence it late had
       arisen.
Sometimes she lingered in towns, till, urged
       by the fever within her,
Urged by a restless longing, the hunger and

thirst of the spirit,
She would commence again her endless search
     and endeaver ;
Sometimes in churchyards stayed, and gaze on
     the crosses and tombstones,
Sat by some nameless grave, and thought that
     perhaps in its bosom
He was already at rest, and she longed to
     slumber beside him.
Sometimems a   rumor, a   hearsay, an
     inarticulate whisper,
Came with its airy hand to point and beckon
     her forward.
Sometimes she spake with those who had seen
     her beloved and known him,
But it was long ago, in some far-off place
or forgotten.
"Gabriel Lajeunesse !" said they ; "O, yes !
     we have seen him.
He was with Basil the blacksmith, and both
     have gone to the prairies ;
Coureur-des-Bois are they, and famous hunters
and trappers."
"Gabriel Lajeunesse !" said others ; "O, yes
! we have seen him,
He is   a **Voyageur** in the lowlands of
     Louisiana."
Then would they say, - "Dear child ! why
     dream and wait for him longer ?
Are there not other   youths as fair as
     Gabriel? others
Who have hearts as tender and true, and
     spirits as loyal ?
Here is Baptiste LeBlanc, the notary's son,
     who has loved thee
Many a tedious year ; come, give him thy hand
     and be happy !
Thou art too fair to be left to braid St.

Catherine's tresses."
Then would Évangéline answer, serenely but
    sadly, - "I cannot !
Whither my heart has gone, there follows my
    hand, and not elsewhere.
For when the heart goes before, like a lamp,
    and illumines the pathway.
Many things are made clear, that else lie
    hidden in darkness."
And thereupon the priest, her friend and
    father-confessor,
Said, with a smile, - "O daughter ! thy God
    thus speaketh within thee !
Talk not of waisted affection, affection
    never was wasted ;
If it enrich not the heart of another, its
    waters, returning
Back to their springs, like the rain, shall
    fill them full of refreshment ;
That which the fountain sends forth returns
    again it the fountain.
Patience ; accomplish thy labor ; accomplish
    thy work of affection !
Sorrow and silence are strong, and patient
    endurance is goodlike.
Therefore accomplish thy labor of love, till
    the heart is made godlike,
Purified, stengthened, perfected, and
    rendered more worthy of heaven !"
Cheered by the good man's words, Évangéline
    labored and waited.
Still in her heart she heard the funeral
    dirge of the ocean,
But with its sound there was mingled a voice
    that whispered, "Despair not !"
Thus did that poor soul wander in want and
    cheerless discomfort,
Bleeding, barefooted, over the shards and
    thorns of existence.

Let   me   easy,   O   Muse !   to   follow   the
        wanderer's footsteps ; -
Not through each devious path, each changeful
        year of existence ;
But   as   a   traveller   follows   a   streamlet's
        course through the valley :
Far from its margin at times, and seeing the
                gleam of its water
Here   and there, in   some open   space, and at
        intervals only ;
Then drawing nearer its banks, through sylvan
        glooms that conceal it,
Though he   behold   it not,   he   can hear   its
        continuous murmur ;
Happy, at length, if we find the spot where
        it reaches an outlet.

11.

It was the month of May. Far down the
        Beautiful River.
Past the Ohio shore and past the mouth of the
        Wabash,
Into the golden stream of the broad and swift
        Mississippi,
Floated a cumbrous boat, that was rowed   by
        Acadian boatmen.
It was a band of exiles : a raft, as it were,
        from the shipwrecked
Nation, scattered along the coast, now
        floating together,
Bound by the bonds of a common belief and a
        common misfortune ;
Men and women and children, who, guided by
        hope or by hearsay,
Sought for their kith and their kin among the
        few-acred farmers
On the Acadian coast, and the prairies of
        fair Opelousas.
With them Évangéline went, and her guide, the
        Father Félicien.
Onward o'er sunken sands, through a
        wilderness sombre with forests,
Day after day they glided adown the turbulent
        river ;
Night after night, by their blazing fires,

encamped on its borders.
Now through rushing chutes, among green
   islands, where plumelike
Cotton-trees nodded their shadowy creasts,
   they swept with the current,
Then emerged into broad lagoons, where
   silvery sand-bars
Lay in the stream, and along the wimpling
   waves of their margin,
Shining with snow-white plumes, large flocks
   of pelicans waded.
Level the landscape grew, and along the
   shores of the river,
Shaded by china-trees, in the midst of
   luxuriant gardens,
Stood the houses of planters, with negro-
   cabins and dove-cots.
They were approaching the region where reigns
   perpetual summer,
Where through the Golden Coast, and groves
   of orange and citron,
Sweeps with majestic curve the river away to
   the eastward.
They, too, swerved from their course ; and,
   entering bayou of Plaquemine,
Soon were lost in a maze of sluggish and
   devious waters,
Which, like a network of steel, extended in
   every direction.
Over their heads the towering and tenebrous
   boughs of the cypress
Met in a dusky arch, and trailing mosses in
   midair
Waved like banners that hang on the walls of
   ancient cathedrals.
Deathlike the silence seemed, and unbroken,
   save by the herons
Home to their roosts in the cedar-trees

returning at sunset,
Or by the owl, as he greeted the moon with
    demoniac laughter.
Levely the moonlight was as it glanced and
    gleamed on the water,
Gleamed on the columns of cypress and cedar
    sustaining the arches,
Down through whose broken vaults it fell as
    through chinks in a ruin.
Dreamlike, and indistinct, and strange were
    all things arounmd them ;
And o'er their spirits there came a feeling
    of wonder and sadness, -
Stange forebodings of ill, unseen and that
    cannot be compassed.
As, at the tramp of a horse's hoof on the
    turf of the prairies,
Far in advance are closed the leaves of the
    shrinking mimosa,
So, at the hoof-beats of fate, with sad
    forebodings of evil,
Shrinks and closes the heart, ere the stroke
    of doom has attained it.
But Évangéline's heart was sustained by a
    vision, that faintly
Floated before her eyes, and beckoned her on
    through the moonlight.
It was the thought of her brain that assumed
    the shape of a phantom.
Through those shadowy aisles had Gabriel
    wandered before her,
And every stroke of the oar now brought him
    nearer and nearer.

Then, in his place, at the prow of the boat,
    rose one of the oarsmen,
And, as a signal sound, if others like them
    peradventure

Sailed on those gloomy and midnight streams,
    blew a blast on his bugle.
Wild   through   the   dark   colonnades   and
    corridors leafy the blast rang,
Breaking the seal of silence, and giving
    tongues to the forest.
Soundless above them the banners of moss just
    stirred to the music.
Multitudinous   echoes awoke and died in the
    distance,
Over   the   watery   floor, and   beneath   the
    reverberant branches ;
But not a voice replied ; no answer came from
    the darkness ;
And when the echoes had ceased, like a sense
    of pain was the silence.
Then Évangéline slept ; but the boatmen rowed
    through the midnight,
Silent   at   times,   then   singing   familiar
    Canadian boat-songs,
Such   as   they   sang   of   old   on their   own
    Acadian rivers.
And   through   the   night   were   heard   the
    mysterious sounds of the desert,
Far   off, indistinct, as   of wave   or wind in
    the forest,
Mixed with the whoop of the crane and the
    roar of the grim alligator.

Thus ere another noon they emerged from those
    shades ; and before them
Lay, in the golden sun, the lakes of the
    Atchafalaya.
Water-lilies in myriads rocked on the slight
    undulatuions
Made by the passing oars, and, respleendent
    in beauty, the lotus

Lifted her golden crown above the heads of
      the boatmen.
Faint was the air with the odorous breath of
      magnolia blossoms,
And with the heat of noon ; and numberless
      sylvan islands,
Fragrant   and   thickly   embowered   with
      blossoming hedges of roses,
Near to whose shores they glided along,
      invited to slumber.
Soon by the fairest of these their weary oars
      were suspended.
Under the boughs of Wachita willows, that
      grew by the margin,
Safely their boat was moored ; and scattered
      about on the greensward,
Tired with their midnight toil, the weary
      travellers slumbered.
Over them vast and high extended the cope of
      a cedar.
Swinging from its great arms, the trumpet-
      flower and the grapevine
Hung their ladder of ropes aloft like the
      ladder of Jacob,
On whose pendulous stairs the angels
      ascending, descending,
Were the swift humming-birds, that flitted
      from blossom to blossom.
Such was the vision Évangéline saw as she
      slumbered beneath it.
Filled was her heart with love, and the dawn
      of an opening heaven
Lighted her soul in sleep with the glory of
      regions celestial.

Nearer and ever nearer, among the numberless
      islands,
Darted a light, swift boat, that sped away

o'er the water,
Urged on its course by the sinewy arms of
    hunters and trappers.
Northward its prow was turned, to the land of
    the bison and beaver.
At the helm sat a youth, with contenance
    thoughtful and careworn.
Dark and neglected locks overshadowed his
    brow, and a sadness
Somewhat beyond his years on his face was
    legibly written.
Gabriel was it, who, weary with waiting,
    unhappy and restless,
Sought in the Western wilds oblivion of self
    and of sorrow.
Swiftly they glided along, close under the
    lee of the island,
But by the opposite bank, and behind a screen
    of palmettos,
So that they saw not the boat, where it lay
    concealed in the willows,
All undisturbed by the dash of their oars,
    and unseen, were the sleepers ;
Angel of God was there none to awaken the
    slumbering maiden.
Swiftly they glided away, like the shade of
    a cloud on the prairie.
After the sound of their oars on the tholes
    had died in the distance,
As from a magic trance the sleepers awoke,
    and the maiden
Said with a sigh to the friendly priest, - "
    O Father Félicien !
Something says in my heart that near me
    Gabriel wanders.
Is it a foolish dream, an idle and vague
    superstition ?
Or has an angel passed, and revealed the

truth to my spirit ?"
Then, with a blush, she added, - "Alas for my
    credulous fancy !
Unto ears like thine such words as these have
    no meaning."
But made answer the reverend man, and he
    smiled as he answered, -
"Daughter, thy words are not idle ; nor are
    they to me without meaning.
Feeling is deep and still ; and the word that
    floats on the surface
Is as the tossing buoy, that betrays where
    the anchor is hidden.
Therefore trust to thy heart, and to what the
    world calls illusions.
Gabriel truly is near thee ; for not far away
    to the southward,
On the banks of the Têche, are the towns of
    St. Maur and St. Martin.
There the long-absent pastor regain his flock
    and his sheepfold,
Beautiful is the land, with its prairies and
    forests of fruit-trees ;
Under the feet a garden of flowers, and the
    bluest of heavens
Bending above, and resting its dome on the
    walls of the forest.
They who dwell there have named it the Eden
    of Louisiana."

With these words of cheer they arose and
    continued their journey.
Softly the evening came. the sun from the
    western horizon
Like a magician extended his golden wand o'er
    the landscape ;
Twinkling vapors arose ; and sky and water
    and forest

Seemed all on fire at the touch, and melted
    and mingled together.
Hanging between two skies, a cloud with edges
    of silver,
Floated the boat, with its dripping oars, on
    the motionless water.
Filled   was   Évangéline's   heart   with
    inexspressible sweetness.
Touched   by the magic spell, the sacred
    fountains of feeling
Glowed with the light of love, as the skies
    and waters around her.
Then from a neighboring thicket the mocking-
    bird, wildest of singers,
Swinging aloft on a willow spray that hung
    o'er the water,
Shook from his little throat such floods of
    delirous music,
That the whole air and the woods and the
    waves seemed silent to listen.
Plaintive at first, were the tones and sad ;
    then soaring to madness
Seemed they to follow or guide the revel of
    frenzied Bacchantes.
Single notes were then heard, in sorrowful,
    low lamentation ;
Till, having gathered them all, he flung them
    abroad in derision,
As when, after a storm, a gust of wind
    through the tree-tops
Shakes down the rattling rain in a crystal
    shower on the branches.
With such a prelude as this, and hearts that
    throbbed with emotion,
Slowly they entered the Têche, where it flows
    through the green Opelousas,
And through the amber air, above the crest of
    the woodland,

Saw the column   of smoke   that arose   from a
     neighboring dwelling ; -
Sounds of a horn they heard,   and the distant
     lowing of cattle.

111.

Near to the bank of the river, o'ershadowed
     by oaks, from whose branches
Garlands   of   Spanish moss and of mystic
     mistletoe flaunted,
Such as the Druids cut down with golden
     hatchets at Yule-tide,
Stood secluded and still, the house of the
     herdsman. A garden
Girded   it   round about   with a belt of
     luxuriant blossoms,
Filling the air with fragrance. The house
     itself was of timbers
Hewn from the cypress-tree, and carefully
     fitted together.
Large and low was the roof ; and on slender
     columns supported,
Rose-wreathed, vine-encircled, a broad and
     spacious veranda,
Haunt of the humming-bird and the bee,
     extended around it.
At each end of the house, amid the flowers of
     the garden,
Stationed the dove-cots were, as love's
     perpetual symbol,
Scenes of endless wooing, and endless
     contentions of rivals.
Silence reigned o'er the place. The line of

shadow and sunshine
Ran near the tops of the trees ; but the house itself was in shadow,
And from its chimney-top, ascending and slowly expanding
Into the evening air, a thin blue column of smoke rose.
In the rear of the house, from the garden gate, ran a pathway
Through the great groves of oak to the skirts of the limitless prairie,
Into whose sea of flowers the sun was slowly descending.
Full in his track of light, like ships with shadowy canvas
Hanging loose from their spars in a motionless calm in the tropics,
Stood a cluster of trees, with tangled cordage of grape-vines.

Just where the woodlands met the flowery surf of the prairie,
Mounted upon his horse, with Spanish saddle and stirrups,
Sat a herdsman, arrayed in gaiters and doublet of deerskin.
Broad and brown was the face that from under the Spanish sombrero
Gazed on the peaceful scene, with the lordly look of its master.
Round about him were numberless herds of kine, that were grazing
Quietly in the meadows, and breathing the vapory freshness
That uprose from the river, and spread itself over the landscape.
Slowly lifting the horn that hung at his side, and expanding

Fully his broad, deep chest, he blew a blast,
    that resounded
Wildly and sweet and for, through the still
    damp air of the evening.
Suddenly out of the grass the long white
    horns of the cattle
Rose like flakes of foam on the adverse
    currents of ocean.
Silent a moment they gazed, then bellowing
    rushed o'er the prairie,
And the whole mass became a cloud, a shade in
    the distance.
Then, as the herdsman turned to the house,
    through the gate of the garden
Saw he the forms of the priest and the maiden
    advancing to meet him.
Suddenly down from his horse he sprang in
    amazement, and forward
Rushed with extended arms and exclamations of
    wonder ;
When they beheld his face, they recognized
    Basil the blacksmith.
Hearty his welcome was, as he led his guests
    to the garden.
There in an arbor of roses with endless
    question and answer
Gave they vent to their hearts, and renewed
    their friendly embraces,
Laughing and weeping by turns, or sitting
    silent and thoughtful.
Thoughtful, for Gabriel came not ; and now
    dark doubts and misgivings
Stole o'er the maiden's heart ; and Basil,
    somewhat embarrassed,
Broke the silence and said, - " If you came
    by the Atchafalaya,
How have you nowhere encountered my Gabriel's
    boat on the bayous ?"

Over Évangéline's face at the words of Basil
    a shade passed.
Tears came into her eyes, and she said, with
    a tremulous accent, -
"Gone ? is Gabriel gone ?" and, concealing
    her face on his shoulder,
All her o'erburdened heart gave way, and she
    wept and lamented.
Then the good Basil said, - and his voice
    grew blithe as he said it, -
"Be of good cheer, my child ; it is only to-
    day he departed.
Foolish boy ! he has left me alone with my
    herds and my horses.
Moody and restless grown, and tried and
    troubled, his spirit
Could no longer endure the calm of this quiet
    existence.
Thinking ever of thee, uncertain and
    sorrowful ever,
Ever silent, or speaking only of thee and his
    troubles,
He at length had become so tedious to men and
    to maidens,
Tedious even to me, that at length I
    bethought me, and sent him
Unto the town of Adayes to trade for mules
    with the Spaniards.
Thence he will follow the Indian trails to
    the Ozark Mountains,
Hunting for furs in the forests, or rivers
    trapping the beaver.
Therefore be of good cheer ; we will follow
    the fugitive lover ;
He is not far on his way, and the Fates and
    the streams are against him.
Up and away to-morrow, and through the red
    dew of the morning
We will follow him fast, and bring him back

to his prison."

Then glad voices were heard, and up from the
     banks of the river,
Borne aloft on his comarades' arms, came
     Michael the fiddler.
Long under Basil's roof had he lived like a
     god on Olypmus,
Having no other care than dispensing music to
     mortals.
Far renowned was he for his silver locks and
     his fiddle.
"Long live Michael," they cried, "our brave
     Acadian minstrel !"
As they bore him aloft in triumphal procession
     and straightway
Father Félcien advanced with Évangéline,
     greeting the old man
Kindly and oft, and recalling the past, while
     Basil, enraptured,
Hailed with hilarious joy his old companions
     and gossips,
Laughing loud and long, and embracing mothers
     and daughters.
Much the marvelled to see the wealth of the
     ci-devant blacksmith,
All his domains and his herds, and his
     patriarchal demeanor ;
Much they marvelled to hear his tales of the
     soil and the climate,
And of the prairies, whose numberless herds
     were his who would take them ;
Each one thought in his heart, that he, too,
     would go and do likewise.
Thus they ascended the steps, and, crossing
     the airy veranda,
Entered the hall of the house, where already

the supper of Basil
Waited his late return ; and they rested and
    feasted together.

Over   the   joyous feast   the   sudden darkness
    descended.
All   was   silent   without,   and   illuming the
    landscape with silver,
Fair rose the dewy moon and the myriad stars
    but within doors,
Brighter   than   these,   shone   the   faces   of
    friends in the glimmering lamplight.
Then from his station aloft, at the head of
    the table, the herdsman
Poured forth his heart and his wine together
    in endless profusion.
Lighting his pipe, that was filled with sweet
    Natchitoches tobacco,
Thus he spake to his guests, who listened,
    and smiled as they listened ; -
"Welcome once more, my friends, who long
    have been friendless and homeless,
Welcome once more to a home, that is better
    perchance than the old one !
Here no hungry winter congeals our blood like
    the rivers ;
Here no stony ground provokes the wrath of
    the farmer ;
Smoothly the ploughshare runs through the
    soil as a keel through the water.
All the year round the orange-groves are in
    blossom ; and grass grows
More in a single night than a whole Canadian
    summer.
Here, too, numberless herds run wild and
    unclaimed in the prairies ;
Here, too, lands may be had for the asking,
    and forests of timber

With a few blows of the axe are hewn and
     framed into houses.
After your houses are built, and your fields
     are yellow with harvests,
No King George of England shall drive you
     away from your homesteads,
Burning your dwellings and barns, and
     stealing your farms and your cattle."
Speaking these words, he blew a wrathful
     cloud from his nostrils,
While his huge, brown hand came thundering
     down on the table,
So that the guests all started ; and Father
     Félicien astounded,
Suddenly paused, with a pinch of snuff half-
     way to his nostrils.
But the brave Basil resumed, and his words
     were milder and gayer ; -
"Only beware of the fever, my friends, beware
     of the fever !
For it is not like that of our cold Acadian
     climate,
Cured by wearing a spider hung round one's
     neck in a nutshell !"
Then there were voices heard at the door, and
     footsteps approaching
Sounded upon the stairs and floor of the
     breezy veranda.
It was the neighoring Creoles and small
     Acadian planters,
Who had been summoned all to the house of
     Basil the herdsman.
Merry the meeting was of ancient comrades and
     neighbors :
Friend clasped friend in his arms ; all they
     who before were as strangers,
Meeting in exile, became straightway as
     friends to each other.

Drawn by the gentle bond of a common country
      together.
But in the neighboring hall a strain of music
      proceeding
From   the   accordant   stings   of Michael's
      melodious fiddle,
Broke up all further speech. Away, like
      children delighted,
All   things   forgotten beside,   they gave
      themselves to the maddening
Whirl of the dizzy dance, as it swept and
      swayed to the music,
Dreamlike, with beaming eyes and the rush of
      fluttering garments.

Meanwhile, apart, at the head of the hall,
      the priest and the herdsman
Sat, conversing together of past and present
      and future ;
While Évangéline stood like one entranced,
      for within her
Olden memories rose, and loud in the midst of
      the music
Heard she the sound of the sea, and an
      irrepressible sadness
Came o'er her heart, and unseen she stole
      forth into the garden.
Beautiful was the night. Behind the black
      wall of the forest,
Tipping its summit with silver, arose the
      moon. On the river
Fell here and there through the branches a
      tremulous gleam of the moonlight,
Like the sweet thoughts of love on a darkened
      and devious spirit,
Nearer and round about her, the manifold
      flowers of the garden
Poured out their souls in odors, that were

their prayers and confessions
Unto the night, as it went its way, like a
slient Carthusian.
Fuller of fragrance than they, and as heavy
with shadows and night-dews,
Hung the heart of the maiden. the calm and
the magical moonlight
Seemed to inundate her soul with indefinable
longings,
As, through the garden gate, beneath the
brown shade of the oak-trees,
Passed she along the path to the edge of the
measureless prairie.
Silent it lay, with a silvery haze upon it,
and fire-flies
Gleaming and floating away in mingled and
infinite numbers.
Over her head the stars, the thoughts of god
in the heavens,
Shone on the eyes of man, who had ceased to
marvel and worship,
Save when a blazing comet was seen on the
walls of that temple,
As if a hand had appeared and written upon
them, "Upharsin."
And the soul of the maiden, between the stars
and the fire-flies,
Wandered alone, and she cried, -"O Gabriel !
O my beloved !
Art thou so near unto me, and yet I cannot
behold thee ?
Art thou so near me, and yet thy voice does
not reach me ?
Ah ! how often thy feet have trod this path
to the prairie !
Ah ! how often thine eyes have looked on the
woodlands around me !
Ah ! how often beneath this oak, returning

from labor,
Thou hast lain down to rest, and to dream of
    me in thy slumbers.
When shall these eyes behold, these arms be
    folded about thee ? "
Loud and sudden and near the note of a
    whippoorwill sounded
Liek a flute in the woods ; and anon, through
    the neighboring thickets,
Farther and farther away it floated and
    dropped into silence.
"Patience !" whispered the oaks from oracular
    caverns of darkness ;
And, from the moonlit meadow, a sigh
    responded, "To-morrow ! "

Bright rose the sun next day ; and all the
    flowers of the garden
Bathed his shining feet with their tears, and
    anointed his tresses
With the delicious balm that they bore in
    their vases of crystal.
"Farewell !" said the priest, as he stood at
    the shadowy threshold ;
"See that you bring us the Prodigal Son from
    his fasting and famine,
And too, the Foolish Virgin, who slept when
    the bridegroom was coming."
"Farewell ! " answered the maiden, and,
    smiling, with Basil descended
Down to the river's brink, where the boatmen
    already were waiting,
Thus beginning their journey with morning,
    and sunshine, and gladness,
Swiftly they followed the flight of him who
    was speeding before them,
Blown by the blast of fate like a dead leaf
    over the desert.

Not that day, nor the next, nor yet the day
    that succeded,
Found they trace of his course, in lake or
    forest or river,
Nor, after many days, had they found him ;
    but vague and uncertain
Rumors alone were their guides through a wild
    and desolate country ;
Till, at the little inn of the Spanish town
    of Adayes,
Weary and worn, they alighted, and learned
    from the garrulous landlord
That on the day before, with horses and
    guides and companions,
Gabriel left the village, and took the road
    to the prairies.

1V.

Far in the West there lies a desert land,
      where the mountains
Lift, through perpetual snows, their lofty
      and luminous summits.
Down form thier jagged, deep ravines, where
      the gorge, like a gateway,
Opens a passage rude to the wheels of the
      emigrant's wagon,
Westward the Oregon flows and the Walleway
      and Owyhee.
Eastward, with devious course, among the
      Windriver Mountains,
Through the Sweet-water Valley precipitate
      leaps the Nebraska ;
And to the south, from Fontaine-qui-bout and
      the Spanish sierras,
Fretted with sands and rocks, and swept by
      the wind of the desert,
Numberless torrents, with ceaseless sound,
      descend to the ocean,
Like the great chords of a harp, in loud and
      solemn vibrations.
Spreading between these streams are the
      wondrous, beautiful prairies,
Billowy bays of grass ever rolling in shadow
      and sunshine,
Bright with luxuriant clusters of roses and
      purple amorphas.
Over them wander the buffalo herds, and the
      elk and the roebuck ;
Over then wander the wolves, and herds of

riderless horses ;
Fires that blast and blight, and winds that
    are veary with travel ;
Over them wander the   scattered   tribes of
    Ishmael's children,
Staining the   desert with blood   and   above
    their terrible war-trails
Circles   and   sails   aloft,   on   pinions
    magestick, the vulture,
Like the implacable soul of a chieftain
    slaughtered in battle,
By invisible stairs ascending and scaling the
    heavens.
Here and there rise smokes from the camps of
    these savage marauders ;
Here and there rise groves from the margins
    of swif-running rivers ;
And   the grim, taciturn bear, the anchorite
    monk of the desert,
Climbs down   their dark ravines to dig for
    roots by the brook-side,
And over all is the sky, the clear and
    crystalline heaven,
Like the protecting hand of God inverted
    above them.

Into this wonderful land, at the base of the
    Ozark Mountains,
Gabriel far had entered, with hunters and
    trapers behind him.
Day after day, with their Indian guidis, the
    maiden and Basil
Followed his flying steps, and thought they
    saw, the smoke of his camp-fire
Rise in the morning air from the diatant
    plain ; but at nightfall,
When   they had reached the place, they found

only embers and ashes.
And, though their hearts were sad at times
and their bodies were weary,
Hope still guided them on, as the magic Fata
Morgana
Showed them her lakes of light, that
retreated and vanished before them.

Once, as they sat by their evening fire,
there silently entered
Into the little camp an Indian woman, whose
features
Wore deep traces of sorrow, and patience as
great as her sorrow.
She was a Shawnee woman returning home to her
people,
From the far-off hunting-grounds of the cruel
Comanches,
Where her Canadian husband, a Coureur-des-
Bois, had been murdered.
Touched were their hearts at her story, and
warmest and friendliest welcome
Gave they, with words of cheer, and she sat
and feasted among them
On the buffalo-meat and the venison cooked on
the embers.
But when their meal was done, and Basil and
all his companions,
Worn with the long day's march and the chase
of the deer and the bison,
Stretched themselves on the ground, and slept
where the quivering fire-light
Flashed on their swarthy cheeks, and their
forms wrapped up in their blankets,
Then at the dood of Évangéline's tent she sat
and repeated
Slowly, with soft, low voice, and the charm
of her Indian accent,

All the tale of her love, with its pleasures,
    and pains, and reverses.
Much Évangéline wept at the tale, and to know
    that another
Hapless heart like her own had loved and had
    been disappointed.
Moved to the depths of her soul by pity and
    woman's compassion,
Yet in her sorrow pleased that one who had
    suffered was near her,
She in turn related her love and all its
    disasters.
Mute with wonder the Shawnee sat, and when
    she had ended
Still was mute ; but at length, as if a
    mysterious horror
Passed through her brain, she spake, and
    repeated the tale of the Mowis ;
Mowis, the bridegroom of snow, who won and
    wedded a maiden,
But, when the morning came, arose and passed
    from the wigwan,
Fading and melting away and dissolving into
    the sunshine,
Till she beheld him no more, though she
    followed far into the forest.
Then, in those sweet, low tones, that seemed
    like a weird incantation,
Told she the tale of the fair Lilinau, who
    was wooed by a phantom,
That, through the pines o'er her father's
    lodge, in the hush of the twilight,
Breathed like the evening wind, and whispered
    love to the maiden,
Till she followed his green and waving plume
    through the forest,
And never more returned, nor was seen again
    by her people.

Silent with wonder and strange surprise,
    Évangéline listened
To the soft flow of her magical words, till
    the region around her
Seemed like enchanted ground, and her swarthy
    guest the enchanteress.
Slowly over the tops of the Ozark Mountains
    the moon rose,
Lighting the little tent, and with a
    mysterious splendor
Touching the somber leaves, and embracing and
    filling the woodland.
With a delicious sound the brook rushed by,
    and the branches
Swayed and sighed overhead in scarcely
    audible whispers.
Filled with the thoughts of love was
    Évangéline's heart, but a secret,
Subtile sense crept in of pain and indefinite
    terror,
As the cold, poisonous snake creeps into the
    nest of the swallow.
It was no earthly fear. A breath from the
    region of spirits
Seemed to float in the air of night ; and she
    felt for a moment
That, like the Indian maid, she, too, was
    pursuing a phantom.
And with this thought she slept, and the fear
    and the phantom had vanished.

Early upon the morrow the march was resumed ;
    and the Shawnee
Said, as they jouneyed along, - "On the
    western slope of these mountains
Dwells in his little village the Black Robe
    chief of the Mission.
Much he teaches the people, and tells them of

Mary and Jesus ;
Loud laugh their hearts with joy, and weep
    with pain, as they hear him. "
Then, with a sudden and secret emotion,
    Évangéline answered, -
"Let us go to the Mission, for there good
    tidings await us ! "
Thither they turned their steeds ; and behind
    a spur of the mountains,
Just as the sun went doown, they heard a
    murmur of voices,
And in a meadow green and broad, by the bank
    of a river,
Saw the tents of the Christians, the tents of
    the Jesuit Mission.
Under a towering oak, that stood in the
        midst of the village,
Knelt the Black Robe chief with his children.
    A crucifix fastened
High on the trunk of the tree, and
    overshadowed by grapevines,
Looked with its agonized face on the
    multitude kneeling beneath it.
This was their rural chapel. Aloft, through
    the intricate arches
Of its aerial roof, arose the chant of their
    vespers,
Mingling its notes with the soft susurrus and
    sighs of the branches.
Silent, with heads uncovered, the travellers,
    nearer approaching,
Knelt on the swarded floor, and joined in the
    evening devotions.
But when the service was done, and the
    benediction had fallen
Forth from the hands of the priest, like seed
    from the hands of the sower,
Slowly the reverend man advanced to the

strangers, and bade them
Welcome ; and when they replied, he smiled
    with benignant expression,
Hearing the homelike sounds of his mother-
    tongue in the forest,
And, with words of kindness, conducted them
    into the wigwam.
There upon mats and skins they reposed, and
    on cakes of the maize-ear
Feasted, and slaked their thirst from the
    water-gourd of the teacher.
Soon was their story told ; and the priest
    with solemnity answered ; -
"Not six suns have risen and set since
    Gabriel, seated
On this mat by my side, where now the maiden
    reposes,
Told me this same sad tale ; then arose and
    continued his journey ! "
Soft was the voice of the priest, and he
    spake with an accent of kindness ;
But on Évangéline's heart fell his words as
    in winter the snow-flakes
Fall into some lone nest from which the birds
    have departed.
"Far to the north he has gone," continued the
    priest ; "but in autumn,
When the chase is done, will return again to
    the Mission."
Then Évangéline said, and her voice was meek
    and submissive, -
"Let me remain with thee, for my soul is sad
    and afflicted."
So seemed it wise and well unto all ; and
    betimes on the morrow,
Mounting his Mexican steed, with his Indian
    guides and companions,
Homeward Basil returned, and Évangéline
    stayed at the Mission.

Slowly, slowly, slowly the days succeeded
    each other, -
Days and weeks and months ; and the fields of
    maize that were springing
Green from the ground when a stranger she
    came, now waving above her,
Lifted their slender shafts, with leaves
    interlacing, and forming
Cloisters for mendicant crows and granaries
    pillaged by squirrels.
Then in the golden weather the maze was
    husked, and the maidens
Blushed at each blood-red ear, for that
    betokened a lover,
But at the crooked laughed, and called it a
    thief in the corn-field,
Even the blood-red ear to Évangéline brought
    not her lover.
"Patience !" the priest would say ; "have
    faith, and thy prayer will be answered !
Look at this delicate plant that lifts its
    head from the meadow,
See how its leaves all point to the north, as
    true as the magnet ;
This is the compass-flower, that the finger
    of God has suspended
Here on its fragile stalk, to direct the
    traveller's journey
Over the sea-like, pathless, limitless waste
    of the desert.
Such in the soul of man in faith. The
    blossoms of passion,
Gay and luxuriant flowers, are brighter and
    fuller of fragrance,
But they beguile us, and lead us astray, and
    their odor is deadly.

Only this humble plant can   guide us here,
    and hereafter
Crown us with asphodel flowers, that are wet
    with the dews of nepenthe."

So came the autumn, and passed, and the
    winter, - yet Gabriel came not ;
Blossomed the opening spring, and the notes
    of the robin and blue-bird
Sounded sweet upon wold and in wood, yet
    Gabriel come not.
But on the breath of the summer winds a rumor
    was wafted
Sweeter than song of bird, or hue or odor of
    blossom.
Far to the north and east, it said, in the
    Michigan forests,
Gabriel had his lodge by the banks of the
    Saginaw river.
And, with retuning guides, that sought the
    lakes of St. Lawrence,
Saying a sad farewell, Évangéline went from
    the Mission.
When over weary ways, by long and perilous
    marches,
She had attained at length the depths of the
    Michigan forests,
Found she the hunter's lodge deserted and
    fallen to ruin !

Thus did the long sad years glide on, and in
    seasons and places
Divers and distant far was seen the wandering
    maiden ; -
Now in the tents of grace of the meek
    Moravian Missions,
Now in the noisy camps and the battle-fields

of the army,
Now in secluded hamlets, in towns and populous cities.
Like a phantom she came, and passed away unremembered.
Fair was she and young, when in hope began the long journey ;
Faded was she and old, when in disappointment it ended.
Each succeeding year stole something away from her beauty,
Leaving behind it broader and deeper, the gloom and the shadow.
Then there appeared and spread faint streaks of gray o'er her forehead,
Dawn of another life, that broke o'er her earthly horizon,
As in the eastern sky the first faint streaks of the morning.

V.

In that delightful land which is washed   by
 the Delaware's waters,
Guarding in sylvan shades the names of Penn
 the apostle,
Stands on the banks of its beautiful stream
 the city he founded.
There all the air is balm, and the peach is
 the emblem of beauty,
And the steets still reëcho the names of the
 trees of the forest,
As if they fain would appease the Dryads
 whose haunts they molested.
There from the troubled sea had Évangéline
 landed, an exile,
Finding among the children of Penn a home and
 a country.
There old René LeBlanc had died ; and when he
 departed
Saw at his side only one of all his hundred
 descendants.
Something at least there was in the friendly
 streets of the city,
Sometheing that spake to her heart, and made
 her no longer a stranger ;
And her ear was pleased with the Thee and
 Thou of the Quakers,
For it recalled the past, the old Acadian
 country,
Where all men were equal, and all were
 brothers and sisters.

So,   when   the   fruitless   search,   the
     disappointed endeavor,
Ended, to recommence no more upon earth,
     uncomplaining,
Thither, as leaves to the light, were turned
     her thoughts and her footsteps.
As from a mountain's top the rainy mists of
     the morning
Roll away, and afar we behold the landscape
     below us,
Sun-illumined, with shining rivers and cities
     and hamlets,
So fell the mists from her mind, and she saw
     the world far below her,
Dark no longer, but all illumined with love ;
     and the pathway
Which she had climbed so far, lying smoothe
     and fair in the distance.
Gabriel was not forgotten. Within her heart
     was his image,
Clothed in the beauty of love and youth, as
     last she beheld him,
Only more beautiful made by his deathlike
     silence and abscence.
Into her thoughts of him time entered not,
     for it was not.
Over him years had no power ; he was not
     changed, but transfigured ;
He had become to her heart as one who is
     dead, and not absent ;
Patience and abnegation of self, and devotion
     to others,
This was the lesson a life of trial and
     sorrow had taught her.
So was her love diffused, but, like to some
     odorous spices,
Suffered no waste nor loss, though filling
     the air with aroma.

Other hope had she none, nor wish in life,
but to follow
Meekly, with reverent steps, the sacred feet
of her Saviour.
Thus many years she lived as a Sister of
Mercy ; frequenting
Lonely and wretched roofs in the crowded
lanes of the city,
Where distress and want concealed themselves
from the sunlight,
Where disease and sorrow in garrets
languished neglected.
Night after night, when the world was asleep,
as the watchman repeated
Loud, through the gusty streets, that all was
well in the city,
High at some lonely window he saw the light
of her taper.
Day after day, in the gray of the dawn, as
slow through the suburbs
Plodded the German farmer, with flowers and
fruits for the market,
Met he that meek, pale face, returning home
from its watchings.

Then it came to pass that a pestilence fell
on the city,
Presaged by wondrous signs, and mostly by
flocks of wild pigeons,
Darkening the sun in their flight, with
naught in their craws but an acorn.
And, as the tides of the sea arise in the
month of September,
Flooding some silver strean, till it spreads
to a lake in the meadow,
So death flooded life, and, o'erflowing its
natural margin,
Spread to a brackish lake, the silver stream

of existence.
Wealth had no power to bribe, nor beauty to
    charm, the oppressor ;
But all perished alike beneath the scourge of
    his anger ; -
Only,   alas ! the poor, who had neither
    friends nor attendants,
Crept away to die in the almshouse, home of
    the homeless.
Then in the suburbs it stood, in the midst of
    meadows and woodlands ; -
Now the city surrounds it ; but still, with
    its gateway and wicket
Meek, in the midst of splendor, its humble
    walls seem to echo
Softly the words of the Lord ; - "The poor ye
    always have with you."
Thither, by night and by day, came the Sister
    of Mercy. The dying
Looked up into her face, and thought, indeed,
    to behold there
Gleams of celestial light encircle her
    forehead with splendor,
Such as the artist paints o'er the brows of
    saints and apostles,
Or such as hangs by night o'er a city seen at
    a distance.
Unto their eyes it seemed the lamps of the
    city celestial,
Into whose shining gates erelong their
    spirits would enter.

Thus, on a Sabbath morn, through the streets
    deserted and silent,
Wending her quiet way, she entered the door
    of the almshouse.
Sweet on the summer air was the odor of

flowers in the garden ;
And she paused on her way to gather the
    fairest among them,
That the dying once more might rejoice in
    their fragrance and beauty.
Then, as she mounted the stairs to the
    corridors, cooled by the east wind,
Distant and soft on her ear fell the chimes
    from the belfry of Christ Church,
While, intermingled with these, across the
    meadows were wafted
Sounds of psalms, that were sung by the
    Swedes in their church at Wicaco.
Soft as descending wings fell the calm of the
    hour on her spirit ;
Something within her said, - "At length thy
    trials are ended ;"
And, with light in her looks, she entered the
    chambers of sickness.
Noiselessly moved about the assiduous,
    careful attendants,
Moistening the feverish lip, and the aching
    brow, and in silence
Closing the sightless eyes of the dead, and
    concealing their faces,
Where on their pallets they lay, like drifts
    of snow by the roadside.
Many a languid head, upraised as Évangéline
    entered,
Turned on its pillow of pain to gaze while
    she passed, for her presence
Fell on their hearts like a ray of the sun on
    the walls of a prison.
And, as she looked around, she saw how Death,
    the consoler,
Laying his hand upon many a heart, had healed
    it forever.
Many familiar forms had disappeared in the
    nightime ;

Vacant   their places were,   or filled already
     by strangers.

Suddenly, as if arrested by fear or a feeling
     of wonder,
Still she   stood, with her colorless lips
     apart, while a shudder
Ran   through her frame, and forgotten, the
     floweres dropped from her fingers,
And from her eyes and cheeks the light and
     bloom of the morning.
Then   there escaped from her lips a cry of
     such terrible anguish,
That the dying heard it, and started up from
     their pillows.
On the pallet before her was stretched the
     form of an old man.
Long, and thin, and gray were the locks that
     shaded his temples ;
But, as he lay in the morning light, his face
     for a moment
Seemed to assume once more the forms of its
     earlier manhood ;
So are wont to be changed the faces of those
     who are dying.
Hot and red on his lips still burned the
     flush of the fever,
As if life, like the Hebrew, with blood had
     besprinkled its portals,
That the Angel of Death might see the sign,
     and pass over.
Motionless, senseless, dying, he lay, and his
     spirit exhausted
Seemed to be sinking down through infinite
     depths in the darkness,
Darkness of   slumber and   death, forever
     sinking and sinking.

Then through those realms of shade, in
    multipied reverberations,
Heard he that cry of pain, and through the
    hush that succeeded
Whispered a gentle voice, in accents tender
    and saint-like,
"Gabriel ! O my beloved !" and died away into
    silence.
Then he beheld, in a dream, once more the
    home of his childhood ;
Green Acadian meadows, with sylvan rivers
    among them,
Village, and mountain, and woodlands ; and,
    walking under their shadow,
As in the days of her youth, Évangéline rose
    in his vision.
Tears came into his eyes ; and as slowly he
    lifted his eyelids,
Vanished the vision away, but Évangéline
    knelt by his bedside.
Vainly he strove to whisper her name, for the
    accents unuttered
Died on his lips, and their motion revealed
    what his tongue would have spoken.
Vainly he strove to rise ; and Évangéline
    kneeling beside him,
Kissed his dying lips, and laid his head on
    her bosom.
Sweet was the light of his eyes ; but it
    suddenly sank into darkness,
As when a lamp is blown out by a gust of wind
    at a casement.

All was ended now, the hope, and the fear,
    and the sorrow,
All the aching of heart, the restless,
    unsatisfied longing,
All the dull, deep pain, and constant anguish

of patience !
And, as she pressed once more the lifeless
head to her bosom,
Meekly she bowed her own, and murmured,
"Father, I thank thee !"

Still stands the forest primeval ; but far
away from its shadow,
Side by side, in their nameless graves, the
lovers are sleeping,
Under the humble walls of the little Catholic
churchyard,
In the heart of the city, they lie, unknown
and unnoticed.
Daily the tides of life go ebbing and flowing
beside them,
Thousands of throbbing hearts, where theirs
are at rest and forever,
Thousands of aching brains, where theirs no
longer are busy,
Thousands of toiling hands, where theirs have
ceased from their labors,
Thousands of weary feet, where theirs have
completed their journey !

Still stands the forest primeval ; but under
the shade of its branches
Dwells another race, with other customs and
language.
Only along the shores of the mournful and
misty Atlantic
Linger a few Acadian peasants, whose fathers
from exile
Wandered back to their native land to die in
its bosom.
In the fisherman's cot the wheel and the

loom are still busy ;
Maidens still wear their Norman caps and
their kirtles of homespun,
Amd by the evening fire repeat Évangéline's
story,
While from its rocky caverns the deep-voiced,
neighboring ocean
Speaks, and in accents disconsolate answers
the wail of the forest.

EVANGÉLINE
(Faed.)